8/94

Know Your Hometown History

KNOW YOUR

Hometown History

PROJECTS AND ACTIVITIES

By Abigail Jungreis

FRANKLIN WATTS
New York ★ Chicago ★ London ★ Toronto ★ Sydney

Frontispiece: *A nineteenth-century flour mill in Mora, New Mexico*

Original art by Elissa Della Piana

Photographs copyright ©: Photo Researchers, Inc.: pp. 2 (Renee Lynn), 16 top (Lillian N. Bolstad), 20 (George E. Jones III), 37 top (David Halpern), 37 bottom (Helen Marcus); Gamma-Liaison: pp. 6 (Stephen Brown), 8 (Dirck Halstead), 9 (George Cohen); Vermont Travel Division: pp. 11, 35 top; FPG International: pp. 16 bottom (Nancy A. Butler), 18 (Larry Aiuppy), 27 (Jeffry W. Myers), 51; Randy Matusow: p. 24; New York Convention & Visitor's Bureau: p. 32; Monkmeyer Press Photo: pp. 35 bottom (Mimi Forsyth), 40 (Roger Dollarhide); Legislative Media Services, Salem, OR: p. 41 (Bryan Peterson); The Oral History Center, Cambridge, MA: p. 43; Union Pacific Railroad Museum Collection: p. 50.

Library of Congress Cataloging-in-Publication Data

Jungreis, Abigail.
    Know your hometown history : projects and activities / by Abigail
Jungreis.
        p.   cm.
    Includes bibliographical references (p.   ) and index.
    Summary: Includes creating a contour map and model of your town,
making a "patchwork quilt" of local history, researching the history
of a place name, and preparing family trees and time lines.
    ISBN 0-531-11124-5
    1. United States—History, Local—Study and teaching (Elementary)—
Juvenile literature.   2. Local history—Study and teaching
(Elementary)—Juvenile literature.   [1. Local history.]   I. Title.
E180.J86 1992
973'.071'2—dc20   92-15407 CIP AC

Contents

Aerial view of Harper's Ferry, West Virginia

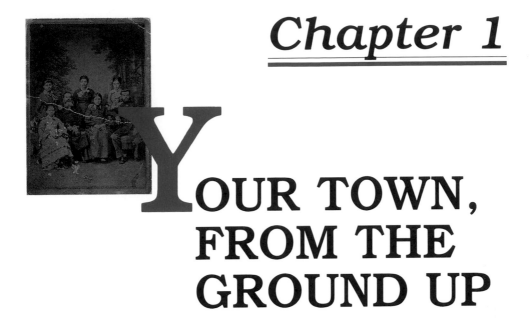

Chapter 1

YOUR TOWN, FROM THE GROUND UP

Have you ever gone looking for history? Maybe you think there is only one place to find it—in a book that describes people and places that are very far away.

Look again. Examine the photo albums in your home. Listen to the stories your family members tell when they gather together. Take a walk down the main street of your community. Notice the statues of famous people from your state. The history of your town and state is all around you.

Finding that history isn't hard, and it can be a lot of fun. This book is full of ideas on how to look for history in your hometown. It includes suggestions on ways to share that history with others. It can help you find out more about your state, your town, even yourself.

You can start your search for history by thinking about where you live. Every community has a history. If you go back far enough, you'll find that history begins with the ground under your feet. Your town or city was built where it is for a reason.

When you are thinking about why something is where it is, you are thinking about its geography. Geography is the study of the environment and people's relationship with it. The environment includes everything around you—plants, animals, water, soil, even the air.

Geography is a key factor in a town's development.
Think of how geography affected the history of
such places as Pittsburgh, Pennsylvania (above) and
Chicago, Illinois (facing page). Find them in an atlas to
learn more about their locations and physical features.

Geography is an important part of history. The location of a place may explain why something happened there. For example, cotton grows well in the warm weather and rich soil of the southern part of the United States. A lot of workers are needed to tend and pick cotton. In the 1800s, some people made slaves do that work. Cold weather in the North prevented the growth of cotton. Northerners had less need to use slaves. This difference in geography helped lead to the Civil War (1861–1865).

Local Geography

To understand the geography of your area, start by identifying its physical features. Physical features are the natural features of the land—for example, rivers, mountains, and forests.

Try this: With a notebook, walk around the area where you live. Ignore the streets, houses, and other buildings. List physical features you see, such as rivers, streams, lakes, hills, or mountains, for example. If there is a park, meadow, or cluster of trees, note them. Write or draw a short description of each entry on your list.

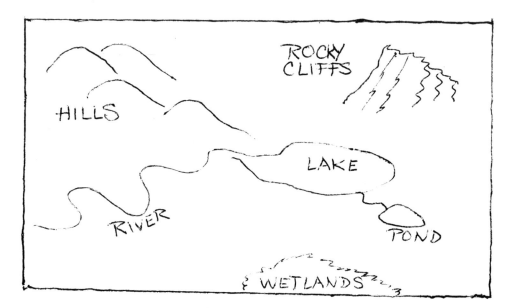

Next, compare your study of local geography with a map. Find a street or road map or atlas (a book of maps) that shows your community. Look for the features you have listed on the map. Did you describe them correctly? Are there features you missed?

Think about the connection between your city, town, or community and the physical features you have noted. Is there a river, lake, or ocean nearby? Many towns are built on bodies of water. Fresh water is important for drinking, and waterfalls have been used to power factories. Water can also be used for transportation. Goods can be moved easily on barges and ships. In the days before railroads, trucks, and airplanes, that was very important. Forests are also important. People have relied on trees for fuel and building material.

Making a Place

Thinking about the physical setting of your town may give you some idea of what it looked like long ago, before settlers from Europe arrived. Only Native Americans lived in

Old covered bridge in Vermont. Settlers in a region find different ways to adapt to its geography.

America then. Your city or town did not exist. Settlers built these towns. They also changed the physical features of the areas they settled. They chopped down trees and wiped out forests. They dammed rivers, creating lakes. In some places, people leveled hills, taking soil from the heights to fill in lower areas.

You can re-create your town's environment by making a model of it.

You will need:

Plasticine

An old baking sheet or pan, (with low sides, as large as possible)

Old sponges or spongeboard

Pebbles

Glue

Think about what you want your model to look like. Do you want hills? Should there be a lake or river? A forest? Where will they go? On a piece of paper draw or note where you want the different physical features to be. Refer to this paper as you build your model.

The baking sheet is your base. Use the plasticine to make the physical features. A mound of plasticine will look like a hill. Push some pebbles into the plasticine and the hill will look rocky. Smooth some plasticine flat and you have a field. A river or lake can be made by digging a channel or hole out of the plasticine and pouring in water.

Shred the sponge into little pieces and press the pieces into the spot where you want trees to be. If you have problems attaching them, use glue.

Plasticine will not harden, so you can change your model until you are happy with the way it looks. After all, you are just doing what people have always done—changing the environment to suit their needs.

Chapter 2

HISTORY AROUND TOWN

Put on a pair of sunglasses and what happens? Everything around you is darker. The sun doesn't glare as much. The world looks different.

Now, use your imagination and put on "historian glasses." Look around your neighborhood and think about its history. Which buildings are old, which are new? Do some have dates or old names on them? Are there statues or monuments in the parks? Are some roads paved with stones, others concrete or asphalt? Do unused railroad tracks run through town?

Once you start looking you can see a lot of history in your neighborhood. With a little bit of detective work, you can find even more.

Inside an old schoolhouse in Kansas. There are probably several
historic sites in your area that you can visit.

Fishermen's Memorial
in Gloucester,
Massachusetts.
Monuments in your
town tell you things
not just about the
events they commemorate,
but about the people
who built them.

Mapping History

Try this: Explore a main street in your neighborhood.

You will need:

A sketchpad

A pencil

Choose an important block in your neighborhood or town. Try to find one with stores on it and also a public building such as the town hall, a school, or the local library.

On your sketchpad, draw two lines like these:

Write the name of the street in between the lines.

MAIN   STREET   ⟶ NORTH

Walk down the sidewalk slowly, noting the buildings on each side of the street on your sketchpad. You can draw squares to show the buildings. Label the squares with the names of the buildings—"Town Hall," "City Savings and Loan," "private house," and "First Church," for example. If there are any monuments or parks on the

Main Street in Wall, South Dakota. Does your town have a main street? How and why was it built?

street, note them, too. If trolley or train tracks go through this street, draw a line showing where these tracks go. By the end of your walk, your sketch might look something like this:

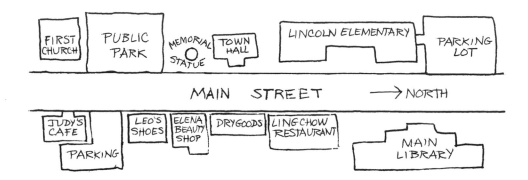

You have just drawn a map! The map tells you about the block today. The next step is to find out about the street's history.

You will need:

Your map of the block

A pencil

Walk down the block again, but this time look closely at the buildings. Do any of them have dates carved into them? Read the signs on the buildings. Church signs often tell you how old a church is. Some businesses proudly display the year they were founded on their signs. Town halls, police headquarters, schools, and other buildings

Dates inscribed in a historic factory in Paterson, New Jersey

run by the government often have engraved cornerstones. These stones, in the front corner of the building, were usually among the first stones placed. They show the date when the building was started. Note all these dates on your map.

Many stores don't have any dates shown on their signs. Even businesses that tell on signs when they were started may not have been in the same building all the time. To investigate the history of those stores, you need to go inside and ask the following questions:

"How long has this business been here?"

"What business was here before yours?"

"When was this building built?"

"What was here before this building?"

If the salesperson doesn't know the answers, try asking a manager or owner. Someone who has worked there for a long time also may be able to give you information on other buildings on the block. Write down the information you get from these conversations on your map. Remember, these people are helping you. Stop in at a quiet time, when there aren't many customers.

Do you know someone who has lived in your neighborhood or town for a long time? Your grandparents or an older neighbor might remember what the street you are exploring was like long ago. Ask them to take a walk with you down the street, and bring along your map. Add their comments and memories to your map.

Become a Tour Guide

Try this: The information on your map will make you a wonderful tour guide. Get a pile of file cards. Write everything you've learned about a building or statue on a file card. Use a different file card for each building. Take your family or class on a tour of the block, reading the correct file card as you come to each building.

Giving a tour of the street is one way to share your

knowledge. Another way is to create a model of how the street looked at some time in the past. Choose a year when you know what the street looked like. Then, using construction paper and different-size boxes, you can create models of the buildings and sights on the street. Attach the file card that describes each building to the model of that building and you can give a tour of the street without leaving the room!

When you do your interview, select a quiet spot, allot adequate time,
and have a list of questions prepared. Some questions might be:
"When you were a child, how did you play?" "What did your parents
do to make a living?" "What was your neighborhood like?"
"How did you stay warm in the winter and cool in the summer?"
"Have you ever seen a U.S. president?"

Chapter 3

SPEAKING OF HISTORY

Have your parents ever said "When I was your age . . . "? Or have you ever heard your grandparents talk about their wedding? Or listened to a next-door neighbor describe a big storm that knocked down all the trees on the block? If you have, you've heard oral history, the spoken stories of individuals.

Historians used to spend most of their time in libraries and archives, opening dusty books and peering at faded records. Those are still great sources of information, especially information from very long ago. But today, many historians are turning to people to find out about the past. By recording an older person recalling personal memories, historians gather important information.

What does it take to be an oral historian? Just a tape recorder, some blank tapes, and the ability to listen.

Doing an Interview

Oral history begins with an interview, talking to someone about his or her memories. No matter who you are interviewing, the same rules apply.

You will need:

☐ A tape recorder. Try to use one with a separate microphone, not one that is built in. Also, a tape recorder that plugs into a socket is better than one that has to run on batteries. Batteries can run out at the worst possible moment!

☐ Blank audiotapes. Always bring more than you think you will need—it would be terrible to miss a great story just because you ran out of tape. Before you even sit down to the interview, label the tape with the date of the interview and the name of the person you are interviewing. Otherwise, you can easily mix up or lose tapes.

☐ A list of questions. Think about what you want to find out. Reporters use a list of question words when they go to cover a story, a list that may help you: Who, What, When, Where, Why, and How. Jot down your questions in a small notebook you can take with you.

☐ A quiet spot. Noise will be picked up by the tape recorder, making it hard to hear the interview. Also, if the room you are in is noisy and busy, the person you are interviewing may be distracted. That person needs to hear your questions and to be able to think about the answers.

☐ Plenty of time. Don't grab a person just as he or she is leaving or about to sit down to dinner. You want them to be relaxed and comfortable, not worried or hungry.

Before you start the interview, test the tape recorder to make sure it's working. Then begin the tape by identifying it. Say: "This is [your name] interviewing [the per-

Create and display a picture archive of your family.

son you're talking to] on [the date] about [whatever subject they are going to talk about]." Even if the label falls off the tape, you will always know when it was recorded and to whom you were speaking. You are also making sure that the person you are speaking to understands and consents to the interview.

Many people feel uncomfortable about speaking into a tape recorder, so start slow. Talk about people you both know, the weather, anything as long as it does not call attention to the tape recorder. When the other person seems relaxed, start asking your questions.

Remember, you are not chatting, you are interviewing. Try to talk as little as possible, and NEVER interrupt.

When you are through, don't turn off the tape recorder that fast. Some of the most interesting information is told at the very end, when the formal interview is over and people are relaxed.

You may need time to get the knack of interviewing. Listen to your early interviews. Is there too much noise in the background? You need to do your interviews in a quieter place. Did you run out of tape? Bring more next time. Did you give the other person enough time to complete a thought? Plan to count to three in your head before you ask another question. That will give the person you interview a chance to add to their answers.

Your Own Project

You can turn your interviewing skill into an oral history project about your community. Start by thinking of a question you want answered.

"What was school like during the time that my grandparents were children?"

"What did people do for fun here 30 years ago?"

"What did the town look like when my parents were my age?"

When you have chosen a question, list the people who might be able to answer it. Your grandparents would be able to answer the first question, for example, but so would other people their age. Your parents can tell you their memories of your town when they were young, but an older shopkccpcr, police officer, or teacher might know even more.

When you have identified the people you think can help you, ask them for an interview. Explain who you are and why you want to speak to them. You may also ask them to suggest other people who can help you. Most people are happy to talk about their memories to someone who seems truly interested.

Going Public

When you complete your interviews, there are many ways you can present the information you gathered. It is always helpful to write down the interviews. You can put the interviews together in a book or you can:

☐ Create a model of what a neighborhood looked like 20 years ago based on the descriptions of older residents.

☐ Draw a mural of the average school day when your grandparents were young.

☐ Make a chart comparing what people do in their spare time today with what they used to do 30 years ago.

You can use oral history skills to research information called for in many of the projects described in this book. You can also use these skills for school reports, or just to satisfy your own curiosity.

Chapter 4

TIES THAT BIND

How many groups do you belong to? You are in a certain class at school—that is one group. Are you on a sports team? That's another. Do you belong to the Scouts? That would be a third.

You may join or leave many different groups every year. But there are other groups you belong to that you will probably never leave: your family, your religion, your ethnic background. These groups are very important in most people's lives. They are also very important to your town, which most likely is made up of people from different families, religions, and backgrounds. Learning the history of these different "communities" will tell you a lot about your hometown.

Finding Your Roots

Have you ever walked by a big, old tree that's been around for a long time? It probably has a strong trunk with many roots you can see and also a lot that you can't. There are old branches near the bottom and younger branches on top. Families grow much as trees do. When a member of

*For immigrants of many backgrounds, Ellis Island (foreground)
in New York harbor was a port of entry during the Great Wave
of Immigration at the turn of the century.*

a family marries and has children, a new branch of the family is formed. When these children have their own children, more branches shoot out.

These similarities may be why your family history is often called your family tree. Finding out about your family's past—where it came from and who your early ancestors were—is known as "finding your roots." Try this: Take a big piece of paper. On one end, put symbols for you, your brothers, and sisters. You may want to use separate symbols for girls (a circle, for example) and boys (a triangle). Underneath each symbol, put names and dates of birth. Then draw a line above your name and put your parents' names and dates of birth. Attach their names to the line showing their children. This is the beginning of your family tree.

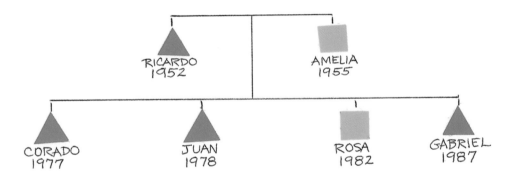

Next, go to your parents and show them the paper. Have them fill in any missing information and then add their brothers and sisters—your aunts and uncles. Children—your cousins—should be underneath their parents. On the line above your parents and aunts and uncles, enter information about your grandparents and their brothers and sisters. Information about their children and grandchildren should go underneath their names. Add those in on the correct lines.

Try to include as much information about each person as you can. Where were your parents and grandparents born? What sorts of work do they do?

Try to get your grandparents (and if you have them, great-grandparents) to check the information, and to fill in any blanks they can. You might be surprised to discover how many generations you can uncover.

Religion in the Community

There are many different religions in this country, and many different houses of worship. They often play an important role in the history of towns and cities.

To find out about the variety of religions in your area, you can start by looking in the telephone directory (yellow pages) under "Churches" (the Christian houses of worship), "Synagogues" (the Jewish houses of worship), "Temples" (for Buddhist and Jewish worship), and "Mosques" (the Muslim houses of worship). You will find listings of places of worship for different religions and particular religious groups, called denominations. Count the number. You may be surprised at how diverse your town is.

Soul Food

What language did your great-great-grandparents speak? How did your ancestors come to this country? Were they here five hundred years ago?

Houses of worship are excellent places to learn more about
local history and the stories of the different groups
who have inhabited your town. Above: *First Church,
Bennington, Vermont.* Below: *A mosque in Tucson, Arizona.*

The answers to these questions tell you about another community you belong to, your ethnic group. Americans are of many different religions and races. Differences in backgrounds affect a number of things, such as the music people listen to and the food they eat.

Food tells a lot about people's background. Rice grows well in much of Asia and it is very nutritious, so people there eat it a great deal. When Asians came to this country, they brought their food preference with them. This is why you will find bags of rice in a Vietnamese grocery store. Most African-Americans were brought to this country to work as slaves. They were given the most inexpensive food to eat, but they came up with wonderful ways to make this food tasty.

Try this: Make a community cookbook.

You will need:

Lined, white paper

Crayons

Two pieces of cardboard, the same size as the paper

Three pipe cleaners

Hole punch (or scissors)

Get a family recipe from your parents or grandparents. Copy the recipe on a clean sheet of paper. Use the crayons to decorate it with designs and pictures that reflect your background. Then ask friends to get recipes from their families. Your friends should copy and decorate these recipes on separate pieces of paper.

Create a cookbook of favorite recipes from your family and friends.

Take one of the pieces of cardboard and title it "The Community Cookbook." This is the front cover of your cookbook, and you may wish to decorate it, too. Gather the recipe pages together and put them between the front cover and the other piece of cardboard, which will be the back cover. Punch three holes in the left-hand side, using the hole punch or scissors. Put a pipe cleaner through each hole, twisting it to form a loop. You have created a cookbook.

You can invite your friends to make the recipes and celebrate with an ethnic feast!

Chapter 5

EXPANDING YOUR COMMUNITY

Think of a toy that babies play with, made of boxes of different sizes. Each box fits snugly into the next biggest box. When they are all stacked, you can see only the biggest box.

That big box is a lot like your state. Inside it, fitting one on top of each other, are the county, town, and neighborhood in which you live. Each one has a history worth exploring.

Send Yourself a Letter

Try this: Get an envelope and address a letter to yourself. Then look at what you have written.

On the first line is your name. Underneath that should be the number of the house and the name of the street on which you live. This line tells people that you live in a particular building in a particular neighborhood. (If it says a post office box, it shows that you live near a certain post office.) A neighborhood could be as small as a group of houses or as large as a great many streets. It is often hard to say where one neighborhood ends and another begins. But people in a neighborhood often feel connected to each other because they live in similar types of homes and shop at many of the same stores.

Now look at the bottom line of your address. It probably starts with the name of a town or a city. These places are official, they have borders and governments. They also provide services—public schools, firefighters, police—to the people who live in them. They come in different sizes and varieties. Cities are large, with lots of people, big buildings, and traffic. Towns, townships, and villages are names of communities that are smaller. A town may be right outside a city, or next to other towns, but each town is distinct from those next to it. Your address will show that.

On some envelopes, the address will show the county in which you live. Most states are divided into counties, which, like cities and towns, have borders. In areas where there are few towns and people live far from each other,

Visit your state library to learn more about your state's history.

The seal of the state of Oregon. Find out about your state's seal and other symbols: the state flag, bird, flower, tree, nickname, and motto. How do they relate to the history of your state?

counties are very important. They provide education and law enforcement and take care of the local roads.

The next thing on your envelope will be the postal abbreviation of your state. States have definite identities. Look up your state in an almanac or encyclopedia. You'll discover that your state has a flag, a motto, and probably even a state song!

What's in a Name?

When people came to the spot you live in, they gave it a name. If they saw a river, lake, or mountains nearby, they named those, too. These names can tell you a lot about the people who have lived in your state.

Try this: Take five pieces of paper. On one piece, write the name of your state. On another, write the name of your city or town. On the top of each of the other three pieces of paper write the name of another important place—your county, for example—or a physical feature nearby: a local mountain, lake, river, or desert.

Now investigate those names. Find out what language the name is in, and what the name means. Colorado, for example, is Spanish for "red." Detroit is French and means "the three." Death Valley is an English name describing a valley that is so hot and dry that many things die in it.

The language of the names tells you from what countries the explorers and settlers of your area came. Some names tell you about the Native Americans who lived there before the settlers came. Connecticut is an Indian word describing the long river that runs through the state. Alaska means "great lands" in the language of Aleuts, a group that has lived in that state for thousands of years.

Sometimes places are named for people. Zebulon Pike was an American explorer who saw Pikes Peak. Seattle is named for an Indian chief, and Virginia for Queen Elizabeth I of England, known as the "Virgin Queen." Was your town, state, or a local hill or river named for a person? Find out about that person, and what he or she did to become famous.

By now, you should know a lot about the name of the places you wrote down. Use that information to draw a picture of what the name tells you about the place. If the place was named for a person, you may want to draw that person. If it's an Indian name, you may draw a picture of what it might have looked like when the Indians lived there. Display the information and the pictures on a large piece of posterboard—and let people know what's in a name.

Scenes from the Past

Once, women used to save all their leftover cloth, which they called "patches." The women put together these pieces of their family's past to make patchwork quilts. You can make your own "patchwork," using pictures from local history.

Patchwork quilt showing stories from girls' and women's lives, from the Oral History Project, Cambridge, Massachusetts

Create a patchwork collage of local history.

Try this: Find out about key events and people in the history of your state, county, town, or neighborhood.

You may want to:

☐ Find out what Native American groups lived in your area five hundred years ago.

☐ Examine your state flag or state seal. Are there people on it? Animals? Is there any writing?

☐ Find out when your state joined the United States. How did that happen?

☐ Identify two people who played important roles in local history. Do research on their lives.

☐ Find out more about an immigrant group that came to your area, any wars that were fought there, a rush for gold or other precious minerals, or a natural disaster.

To find out about this history, you can interview neighbors, go to the library and look at old newspapers, and look up your city or state in the encyclopedia. Your town may have a historical society you can visit.

Now you are ready to create the patches.

You will need:

Colored construction paper, felt, old magazines, old buttons or shoe laces, stickers, and other fun junk

Glue

A pencil

Scissors

Tape

Make at least six of these panels. Tape the panels together in three rows of two panels each. You have created a colorful patchwork—and you also have a picture history of the places in which you live.

Chapter 6

MARK TIME

The more you find out about your town's history, the more you learn about how it has changed. Elections have been held, monuments built, stores closed. There may be more or fewer people in town than ten years ago, but chances are there are not the same number.

Historians study these changes. To do this, they have to know the order in which events occurred. What was built first, the new mall or the new school? Did the mayor lose the election before or after the factory closed down? To do a good hometown history, you have to keep track of time.

A Line into the Past

One of the best ways to put things in the order in which they occurred is to create a time line.
Try this: Make a time line of your town or city.

You will need:

Large long sheet of paper (cut a generous piece off a roll of white wrapping paper)

Black magic marker

Notebook and pencil (for researching)

With the magic marker, draw a long, straight line across the width of the paper. On the left, at the start of the line, write the year the town was started. (You can find out this information in the library or by calling the town or city clerk.) On the right, at the end of the line, write down this year. Divide the line equally, noting each of the years in between.

Now research the history of your town. Start in the library or, if it exists, the local historical society. There may be books or pamphlets about the history of your town. Look through old copies of the local newspaper and note important events.

Ask older people to recall events that affected your community. Go to your parents, a teacher, even an older brother or sister. Jog their memories by asking them:

"Do you remember any big storms, earthquakes, or fires that affected the town?"

"Did any famous or important people visit?"

"Have factories started or closed down?"

Next, enter the events you've collected by the correct date on the time line. You don't have to write down everything that has happened, just the ones that you think are really important.

1820	1847	1860	1864	1892	1919	1937	1957	1992
Old Granite Quarry is mined	Patrolman Wade is a Hero of the Great Fire.	New High School is Built. 1,537 Students. Now the Winthrop Condos.	Civil War claims 7,856 enlistees, and Ultimately 1,200 lives	Wright's Pond and Wildlife Preserve is established.	Mary O'Sullivan is elected Labor and Industries Inspector. A tireless worker for Labor, she helped create the national holiday.	Unemployment is 33% of Male population.	Tufts College becomes Tufts University.	100th Anniversary Parade and Celebration of our City's Incorporation.
Isaac Sprague House is built. He was a pioneer of Education in the United States.	1852- Tufts College is founded by Rev. Tufts.	Streetcar tracks are laid for Horse drawn cars.	1869- Fell's Parkway is set down as a Natural reserve, a track of 4,000 acres.	Amelia Earhart born, 1897. She settled in Medford in 1924. Flew her historic flight across the Atlantic 1928.	1930-Tricentennial.	Baptist and Universalists Churches start a Soup Kitchen. Together serving 7 days a week.	Current High School is built on Main Street. 2,700 students.	City Population is 76,000.
1830 -Bicentennial.	James Pierpont writes "Jingle Bells"	Fulltime Fire Department is Commissioned.	Opera House is Built on Salem Street. This is now the Medford Cinema.	CITY is INCORPORATED Gypsy Moth Epidemic Begins - 1907.	Streetcar tracks are laid from Boston to Arlington through Medford and West Medford.	WWII claims 430 lives, 1944.	Route 93 Interstate is built to connect Medford to Boston Continuing to Canadian Border.	
Drawbridge over Mystic River is Dismantled and Stone bridge built.					First Movie Production Company, Elm Street.		57 Residents qualify for Boston Marathon Korean War claims 174 Medford lives.	
							1978-The Great Blizzard.	

Pieces of the Past

History is more than written descriptions. Historians learn a lot from pictures and documents. Try this: Gather things that can illustrate your town's history. Old issues of the local newspaper will have pictures you can copy. Also your family might have saved old papers that illustrate the history of the town, such as a program from your parents' high school graduation or a postcard from twenty years ago. You can take photographs of a closed factory or new houses.

WARNING! The old photographs and documents you collect are precious. A good historian needs to be very careful with them. Photocopy all papers and photographs. Carefully put the originals away.

Get ahold of some old photos and examine them closely.
This photo is from the archives of the Union Pacific Railroad.

JEMIMA JONES
Passed on Jan 4 1803

This is the last long resting place
of Aunt Jemimas bones
Her soul ascended into space
amidst our tears and groans
She was not pleasing to the eye
nor had she any brain
And when she talkd, twas thru her nose
which gave her friends much pain
But still we feel that she was worth
the money that was spent
Upon the coffin, hearse and stone
(the mourning plumes were lent)

A visit to a local cemetery might reward you with
words such as these. You can also make simple
rubbings of tombstones and cornerstones.

Buildings sometimes have cornerstones, with the date the building was started carved into the stone. You can make a rubbing of that cornerstone. Take a piece of paper and put it over the stone. Then rub a crayon across the paper. The crayon will color everything but where the stone was carved—so you will have a copy of the words on the stone.

Paste the pictures, rubbings, and photocopies above the written entries on your time line. Make sure they're positioned above the correct year. Your time line is complete! Put it on display or carefully store it. You can even add to it as you get older. In the future, when you look at this time line, you will see just how your hometown has changed.

Resources for Research

For a really good map of your area, write to
USGS Map Sales
Box 25286
Denver, CO 80225

For more information on state history, write to one of the following.

Alabama:
State of Alabama
Alabama Tourism and
    Travel
532 Perry Street
Montgomery, AL 36104

Alaska:
Alaska State Library
Department of Education
P.O. Box 6
333 Willoughby Ave.
Juneau, Al 99811

Arizona:
Arizona Historical Society
949 E. 2d St.
Tucson, AZ 85719

Arkansas:
Secretary of State's Office
Information Service
State Capitol
Little Rock, AR 72201

California:
Secretary of the Senate
Room 3044
State Capitol
Sacramento, CA 95814

Colorado:
Colorado Historical
    Society
1300 Broadway
Denver, CO 80203

Connecticut:
Connecticut Historical
    Society
1 Elizabeth Street
Hartford, CT 06105

Delaware:
Historical Society of
    Delaware
505 Market St.
Wilmington, DE 19801

Florida:
Museum of Florida History
500 S. Bronough St.
R. A. Grey Building
Tallahassee, FL 32399-0250

Georgia:
Office of the Secretary of
State
Attn.: Tours Desk
State Capitol
Atlanta, GA 30334

Hawaii:
Hawaii State Library
Hawaii and Pacific Room
478 South King Street
Honolulu, HI 96813

Idaho:
Boise Public Library
715 Capitol Blvd.
Boise, ID 83702

Illinois:
Illinois Historic Preservation
Agency
Old State Capitol
Springfield, IL 62701

Indiana:
Indiana Historical Society
315 W. Ohio St.
Indianapolis, IN 46202

Iowa:
Iowa State Historical
Society
Capitol Complex
Des Moines, Iowa 50319

Kansas:
Kansas State Historical
Society
120 West 10th Street
Topeka, KS 66612

Kentucky:
Kentucky Historical Society
P.O. Box H
Frankfort, KY 40602

Louisiana:
Secretary of State
Archives Division
P.O. Box 94125
Baton Rouge, LA 70804-
9125

Maine:
Maine Historical Society
485 Congress St.
Portland, ME 04101

Maryland:
Maryland Historical Society
201 West Monument St.
Baltimore, MD 21201

Massachusetts:
Department of Commerce
and Development
Division of Tourism
100 Cambridge Street
Boston, MA 02202

Michigan:
Michigan Historical
Museum
208 N. Capital
Lansing, MI 48918

Minnesota:
Minnesota Historical
   Society
690 Cedar Street
St. Paul, MN 35101

Mississippi:
Historical and Genealogical
   Assn. of Mississippi
618 Avalon Road
Jackson, MS 39206

Missouri:
Missouri State Historical
   Society
Lowry and Hitt Sts.
Columbia, MO 65201

Montana:
Historical Society Library
225 North Roberts
Helena, MT 59620

Nebraska:
Nebraska State Historical
   Society
P.O. Box 82554
Lincoln, NE 68501

Nevada:
Nevada State Museum and
   Historical Society
700 Twin Lakes Dr.
Las Vegas, NV 89107

New Hampshire:
New Hampshire Historical
   Society
30 Park St.
Concord, NH 03301

New Jersey:
New Jersey Historical
   Society
230 Broadway
Newark, NJ 07104

New Mexico:
Historical Society of New
   Mexico
P.O. Box 5819
Santa Fe, NM 87502

New York:
New York State Museum
Room 3099
Cultural Education Center
Albany, NY 12230

North Carolina:
School Information Program
State Library
109 East Jones Street
Raleigh, NC 27611

North Dakota:
State Historical Society
Heritage Center
Bismarck, ND 58505

Ohio:
Ohio Historical Center
Educational Services
   Department
1985 Velma Avenue
Columbus, OH 43211

Oklahoma:
Oklahoma State Historical
   Society
2100 N. Lincoln
Oklahoma City, OK 73105

Oregon:
Secretary of State
Oregon Blue Book
State Capitol
Salem, OR 97310

Pennsylvania:
Historical Society of
    Pennsylvania
1300 Locust St.
Philadelphia, PA 19107

Rhode Island:
Rhode Island Historical
    Society
110 Benevolent St.
Providence, RI 02906

South Carolina:
South Carolina Department
    of Archives and History
P.O. Box 11669
1430 Senate Street
Columbia, SC 29211

South Dakota
South Dakota State
    Historical Society
900 Governor's Drive
Pierre, SD 57501

Tennessee:
Tennessee State Library and
    Archives
403 7th Ave N.
Nashville, TN 37219

Texas:
Staff Services
P.O. Box 12428
Austin, TX 78711

Utah:
Division of State History
300 Rio Grande
Salt Lake City, UT 84101

Vermont:
Vermont Historical Society
109 State Street
Montpelier, VT 05609

Virginia:
Virginia Historical Society
P.O. Box 7311
428 N. Blvd.
Richmond, VA 23221

Washington:
Superintendent of Public
    Information
Old Capitol Building
FG-11
Olympia, WA 98504-3211

West Virgina:
Division of Culture
    and History
Capitol Complex-Cultural
    Center
Charleston, WV 25305

Wisconsin:
State Historical Society of
    Wisconsin
816 State St.
Madison, WI 53703

Wyoming:
State Archives Museum and
    Historical Department
604 E 25th St.
Cheyenne, WY 82002

Some useful books:

Gilford, Henry. *Genealogy: How to Find Your Roots,* New York: Franklin Watts, 1978.

Marty, Myron A. and David E. Kyvig. *Nearby History: Exploring the Past Around You.* Nashville: American Association for State and Local History, 1982.

Weitzman, David. *My Backyard History Book.* Boston: Little Brown, 1975.

For information on individual states, see: The New Enchantment of America Series (Chicago: Childrens Press).

INDEX

About the Author

Abigail Jungreis holds a B.A. in history from Princeton University and is a social studies textbook editor at a major publishing house. A Philadelphia native who now lives in Boston, Ms. Jungreis has been a writer and editor for Scholastic Magazines and a reporter for the *Anchorage Daily News.* She likes to row crew, knit, and is involved in a family oral history project.